THE
POLITICAL ECONOMY
OF THE
ARAB UPRISINGS

Melani Cammett and Ishac Diwan

WESTVIEW
PRESS

A Member of the Perseus Books Group

Westview Press was founded in 1975 in Boulder, Colorado, by notable publisher and intellectual Fred Praeger. Westview Press continues to publish scholarly titles and high-quality undergraduate- and graduate-level textbooks in core social science disciplines. With books developed, written, and edited with the needs of serious nonfiction readers, professors, and students in mind, Westview Press honors its long history of publishing books that matter.

Copyright © 2014 by Westview Press

Published by Westview Press,
A Member of the Perseus Books Group

Find us on the World Wide Web at www.westviewpress.com.

Every effort has been made to secure required permissions for all text, images, maps, and other art reprinted in this volume.

Westview Press books are available at special discounts for bulk purchases in the United States by corporations, institutions, and other organizations. For more information, please contact the Special Markets Department at the Perseus Books Group, 2300 Chestnut Street, Suite 200, Philadelphia, PA 19103, or call (800) 810-4145, ext. 5000, or e-mail special.markets @perseusbooks.com.

A CIP catalog record for the print version of this book is available from the Library of Congress
ISBN 978-0-8133-4944-2 (paperback)
ISBN 978-0-8133-4945-9 (e-book)

THE POLITICAL ECONOMY OF THE ARAB UPRISINGS

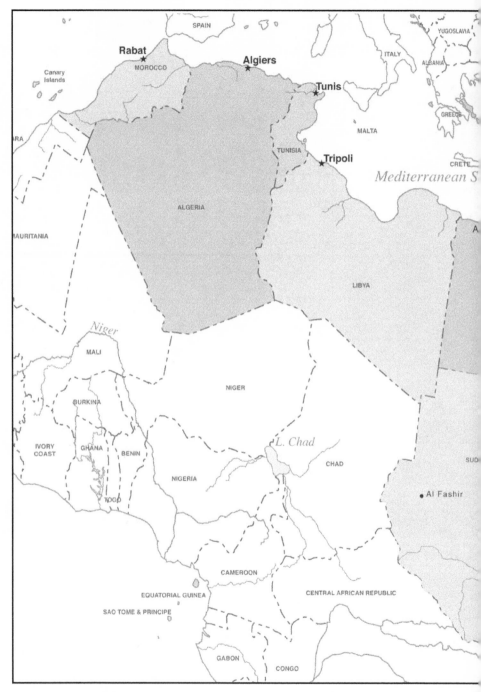

Map 0.1   The Middle East and North Africa

THE POLITICAL ECONOMY
OF THE ARAB UPRISINGS

Since the last edition of this book was published, revolutionary movements have swept across the Middle East. The "Arab Spring" began on December 17, 2010, in Tunisia, where Mohamed Bouazizi, a vegetable seller in the central Tunisian town of Sidi Bouzid, set himself on fire to protest mistreatment by local police and government authorities. Bouazizi's act incited a wave of protests, beginning in rural areas and later spreading to urban coastal areas, which encompassed a diverse array of participants ranging from informal-sector workers, like Bouazizi himself, to unemployed graduates, workers, lawyers, and cyber-connected youth. Ultimately, these mass protests led to the ouster of Zine al-Abdine Ben 'Ali, who had ruled Tunisia in an increasingly repressive manner for over two decades. Protesters demanded justice and accountability from their government and refused to step down, even in the face of brutal repression and government promises to create new jobs and to expand civil and political liberties.

The revolutionary movement then spread to Egypt, where Hosni Mubarak, who had held power for almost thirty years, was ousted after several weeks of protests in Cairo and other cities. In Egypt, too, protesters remained steadfast in the face of a harsh crackdown, calling for Mubarak and his key henchmen to step down. In February 2011, Mubarak resigned and later faced trial for complicity in the murder of protesters. From Tunisia and Egypt, protests spread across the region to Yemen, Algeria, Libya, Syria, Jordan, Bahrain, and even Saudi Arabia. More sporadic and, in some cases, short-lived protests took place in Morocco, Iraq, Lebanon, and Palestine.

Revolutions and rebellions are complex phenomena. Likewise, the motivations for the Arab uprisings are multifaceted. Political concerns, such as outrage over dictatorial rule, repression, and restrictions on basic liberties were undoubtedly important. For many people, however, economic issues were equally if not more salient. A 2005 poll conducted by Zogby International found that expanding employment opportunities, improving the health care and educational systems, and ending corruption were the most important priorities of citizens across the region. Democracy and civic and political rights, though also cited, were ranked lower than socioeconomic concerns (Zogby International 2005). Similarly, the 2010 Arab Youth Survey found that the greatest perceived challenge and concern of Arab youth was the cost of living, followed by unemployment and then human rights. The largest *change* relative to the previous survey, which was conducted one year earlier, was the increased perception of income inequality (ASDA'A/Burson-Marsteller 2010).

More fundamentally, it is difficult to extricate the economic and political motivations for the uprisings given the evolution of Arab political economies over the past few decades. The rise of crony capitalism, which we discuss later in the chapter, underscores the ways in which politics and, more specifically, political connections have shaped economic opportunities in the region. As implied by the slogan "Bread, freedom, and social justice," which protesters chanted on Avenue Bourguiba and in Tahrir Square and elsewhere in the region, inequality of opportunity was a central concern. Thus, a political economy approach has much to contribute to interpretations of the initial motivations for the uprisings and of the dynamics of ongoing political and economic transitions.

Despite momentous political changes in the region, many insights from the third edition of this book, which was published over two years before Bouazizi set himself on fire, remain relevant. Some of the core economic and political challenges described in the book were important factors that either directly or indirectly contributed to the uprisings. Richards and Waterbury pointed to insufficient job creation, labor market pressures exacerbated by the youth bulge, the mismatch between educational systems and labor market needs, the declining quantity of water and rising dependency on food imports, the continuing decay of the public sector, the mixed record of economic liberalization, a growing housing crisis in urban areas, and the rise of political Islam across the region.

The Arab Spring also created new developments that cannot be fully appreciated without new analytical tools that were not in earlier editions of this book. With ousted leaders and struggles over the construction of new political institutions in some countries, the classification of regime types in the region must be revised. Even in countries where incumbent rulers remain entrenched, the nature of the political game has changed. Across the region, "street politics" is an increasingly important form of political expression and citizens are making more forceful and more frequent demands on their leaders. At this juncture, the context of policymaking is altered: New political regimes are emerging, and with the rise of claim-making, rulers are compelled to respond more effectively to citizen demands. Evolving political systems as well as economic developments demand new perspectives on the political economies of the region.

The Arab uprisings also highlight issues that require more in-depth analysis than prior editions of this book emphasized. In particular, the perceived increase in inequalities, discontent with public services, the political economy of cronyism, the narrowing composition of authoritarian coalitions, and succession issues in Arab republics have proven to be important developments across the Arab world.

What explains the origins and dynamics of the Arab uprisings? We believe that a political economy approach has much to offer in addressing this question. Neither purely political concerns, such as the desire of populations for democracy, nor simple economic trends can explain the decisions of protesters to call for the downfall of autocratic rulers. Rather, the interaction of political factors and real and perceived economic developments brought about the uprisings. As we argue later, narrowing authoritarian coalitions in the context of crony capitalism, the rollback of the state, and declining welfare regimes alienated formal-sector workers and tenuous middle classes. In the context of unequal life chances and rising insecurity, growing portions of Arab societies perceived that the inequality of opportunities was on the rise. Thus, neither growth rates nor absolute levels of income inequality can account for popular movements to overthrow incumbent dictators. Rather, *perceptions* of socioeconomic trends in the context of evolving political economies were at the root of mass protests.

In this epilogue, we develop these claims in more detail. First, we sketch out a picture of regional variation in the uprisings, pointing to a variety of factors that differentiate the countries of the region and help to explain their distinct trajectories thus far during this period of momentous change. The following section develops a framework for understanding the uprisings. The final part focuses on the dynamics of the transitions across the Middle East, analyzing the ways in which political and economic factors are interacting to shape the construction of new political institutions and economic reform programs.

CROSS-REGIONAL VARIATION IN THE ARAB UPRISINGS

The outcomes of the uprisings thus far have varied across the Arab world. In some countries, such as Tunisia, Egypt, and Libya, rulers have been deposed and political actors are engaged in struggles over the creation of new institutional rules. In Yemen, regime change occurred through a more "pacted" transfer of power negotiated by elites, although mass mobilization initially precipitated the ouster of former president 'Ali 'Abdullah Salih. In February 2012, voters endorsed a deal brokered by the Gulf Cooperation Council, approving a two-year transitional presidency for Salih's vice president of eighteen years, 'Abd Rabbo Mansour Hadi.

In other countries, regimes have pushed back decisively against protesters. In Syria, the regime's harsh crackdown on initial protests sparked a bloody conflict that continues unabated as of this writing. In Bahrain, too, the ruling al-Khalifa family has harshly repressed protesters who are calling for regime change, although far less blood has been spilled than in Syria. The international community has responded in divergent ways to the crises in Syria and Bahrain. Direct intervention from neighboring Saudi Arabia and limited condemnation from the United States, which has a strategic alliance with Bahrain, have bolstered the ruling family's control. The United States and other countries have hesitated to intervene directly in Syria, in part because of Russian opposition to international involvement and in part because of stated concerns about the fragmentation of the opposition and the role of Islamist extremists in the armed opposition to the As'ad regime.

Not all uprisings in the Arab world have culminated in or even called for the dismissal of authoritarian rulers. In some countries, sustained protests were met with concessions by rulers. In Jordan, protesters by and large have not demanded an end to the monarchy but rather have issued demands for increased economic opportunities and greater freedoms under the current system. In response, King Abdullah replaced the prime minister multiple times and called early elections, although these moves have failed to appease the opposition. In Morocco, King Muhammad VI pledged to introduce greater political freedoms and held a referendum on constitutional reforms that ostensibly reduced the power of the monarch but, in practice, brought about little substantive change in the system (Benchemsi 2012). At this juncture, protests have abated in Morocco, but if the king's alleged commitment to gradual reform does not bring about significant change, they could reignite. Protests of varying scales and durations have also erupted in Algeria, Iraq, and Lebanon, compelling rulers to make some real and some rhetorical concessions. The fragmentation of political systems and exhaustion after prolonged conflicts in these countries, however, have hampered the ability of opposition movements to gain traction and bring about meaningful reform.

Opposition groups have even staged protests in the wealthy Arab Gulf monarchies. In Kuwait, which has a comparatively long history of political contestation, the parliament was dissolved and the prime minister was replaced. In general, however, protests have been more limited and short-lived across the Gulf. In most cases, incumbent rulers have taken advantage of high oil prices to quell protests through economic incentives.

Several basic economic and political factors differentiate the countries of the region, explaining some of the variation in the trajectories of the Arab uprisings. Oil wealth is the most obvious distinction among Arab countries. In the oil-rich countries with low populations, the autocratic bargain—material benefits in exchange for political quiescence—can still function owing to high oil rents. To be sure, oil is not determinative and cannot explain all politics in the Gulf, as the case of Kuwait demonstrates. At a minimum, high per capita oil wealth enables rulers to postpone serious challenges to their authority and may even prevent the emergence or spread of opposition groups in the first place.

The extent of ethnoreligious diversity and, most importantly, politicized identity-based cleavages also accounts for some variation in the dynamics of the uprisings across the Arab countries. Particularly in the Levant, notably Syria, Iraq, Lebanon, and, to a lesser degree, Jordan, ethnoreligious politics has shaped the demands of opposition groups and the course of the protests. Autocratic coalitions have historically favored some groups over others, a strategy of political control that dates back to the colonial period and continued after independence. In some of these countries, rulers incorporated minorities, who fear the tyranny of majorities. For example, in Syria, the majority Sunni population has been less privileged than Alawis and other minority groups, although Sunni elites have prospered under the As'ad family's rule as well. The Hashemite monarchy in Jordan has historically favored East Bank "Transjordanian" tribes and families, rewarding them with positions in the civil service and military that come with job security and benefits, while Jordanians of Palestinian origin tend to dominate the private sector and the informal economy.

The uprisings have undermined or destabilized core political settlements and have sometimes resulted in violence. The struggle in Syria is increasingly described in sectarian terms, with an opposition that is overwhelmingly Sunni pitted against a minority Alawi regime. The dynamics of protest in Bahrain are also depicted as sectarian: the ruling al-Khalifa family, a Sunni monarchy ruling over a majority Shi'a population, has used harsh repression to put down the largely Shi'a opposition. The uprisings have even upset the balance in comparatively stable Jordan: with economic deterioration, the monarchy's core Transjordanian constituency is increasingly disgruntled and more sympathetic to the opposition movement.

It is vital to emphasize, however, that an interpretation of political struggles based on sectarian grievances vastly oversimplifies political and economic realities in Bahrain, Syria, and other countries in the region. Ethnoreligious cleavages per se do not necessarily produce conflict (Brubaker 2006; Chandra 2012; Fearon and Laitin 1996; Lieberman and Singh 2012). Rather, identity-based differences must be politically salient in order to become a basis for political mobilization. A surefire way to activate ethnoreligious identity is to distribute resources along ostensibly identity-based lines. For example, in Iraq, most people did not prioritize their identities as Shi'a or Sunni Muslims until well into the twentieth century (Jabar 2003). Saddam Hussein's policies and, more generally, the breakdown of the state during the sanctions period and following the US invasion in 2003 were instrumental in activating religious identities in Iraq. Saddam increasingly favored Sunnis, especially those from his native town of Tikrit, and repressed the Shi'a, whose religious networks posed a threat to his rule. As a result, the Shi'a felt marginalized in Saddam's Iraq, and Shi'a political leaders have taken advantage of his overthrow to consolidate their authority. But even in Iraq, where sectarianism appears to define political life, some of the most intense conflict occurs among coreligionists. Political competition is particularly intense among different Shi'a groups and has even erupted in violence.

Finally, regime type appears to explain some differences in the nature and intensity of uprisings across the Arab world, although closer inspection may reveal this to be a spurious correlation. The record suggests that the monarchies have been less vulnerable to demands for regime change and have even witnessed less sustained opposition movements. As noted earlier, per capita oil wealth is part of the reason for the more muted nature of the uprisings in many monarchies; it cannot, however, account for the Jordanian and Moroccan cases. To explain their longevity, monarchs in Jordan and Morocco emphasize their legitimacy, an argument that is more convincing for Morocco, where the monarchy has been in place since the seventeenth century, than for Jordan, which was a colonial construction (Massad 2001). But even in Morocco, legitimacy is an unconvincing explanation, in part because it is vague and difficult to measure and in part because there was nothing inevitable about the monarchy's survival and perpetuation in the post-independence period. Rather, the structure of patronage helps to explain why monarchies have been less destabilized than republics in the Arab uprisings. In particular, monarchies have tended to establish multifaceted authoritarian coalitions, broadening their support base in society and reducing the potential demand for their overthrow (Yom and Gause 2012). Thus, rather than regime type per se, the structure of authoritarian coalitions in monarchies versus republics provides a more convincing account for the varied trajectories of uprisings in the Arab world today.[1] This is why the rising grievances among Transjordanians, a key part of the authoritarian coalition in Jordan, are particularly worrisome for the Hashemite monarchy.

Our emphasis on the composition of authoritarian coalitions in explaining both the durability and the breakdown of authoritarian rule points to the broader value of a political economy approach for understanding the emergence and progression of uprisings in the Arab countries. In the next section, we spell out the core elements of such an approach.

PROLONGED DISCONTENT: THE SOCIOECONOMIC FOUNDATIONS OF THE ARAB UPRISINGS

Many of the characteristics of the recent Arab uprisings are puzzling and do not fit easily within popular intellectual frames. Why did they occur at the end of 2010, when there were no apparent direct triggers such as declines in subsidies or shifts in foreign alliances, rather than in the 1990s, when the welfare state began to be rolled back? Why did the revolutions start in Tunisia and Egypt, the countries with some of the highest economic growth in the region in the preceding few years, rather than in countries such as Syria or Yemen, where economic conditions were more dire and political repression more severe? Why were they initiated by secularist middle-class youth, the supposed beneficiaries of the modernizing republics, rather than by the long-standing Islamist opposition?

In the early days of the Arab Spring, debates about the relative importance of economic versus political factors permeated journalistic and scholarly discussions about the motivations for the mass protests across the region. On the face of it, economic factors hold little explanatory value. In the preceding decade, economic growth was not low in the "revolution" countries, at about 4 to 5% of GDP per year: in 2010, growth stood at 3.1% in Tunisia, 5.1% in Egypt, 3.4% in Syria, 3.7% in Libya, 7.7% in Yemen, 3.7% in Morocco, and 2.3% in Jordan (World Bank, *World Development Indicators,* 2010). The macroeconomic situation was also relatively stable after the imbalances of the early 2000s were absorbed, with shrinking budget and current account deficits and reasonable debt levels. On the eve of the uprisings, international reserves were at comfortable levels. The unemployment rate was high in most Arab countries, between 10 and 15% of the labor force, higher than in other developing regions, but stable. Inequality as measured by GINI coefficients was lower than in other regions, with values at around 0.3 to 0.4, and was not rising fast (Belhaj and Wissa 2011).

To be sure, the 2008 global recession, coupled with the oil and food crises, did affect the region. Growth slowed down after 2008, and while it had recovered somewhat by 2010, it remained below the levels reached in 2006 to 2008. Energy subsidies increased with international prices, further eroding the ability of the state to spend on public investment and wages, while inflation rose and real wages fell. Furthermore, rising growth rates in the 2000s were unable to reach Asian double-digit levels, which would have been needed to absorb the youth wave and the unemployed in the labor market. In cross-regional comparative perspective, youth unemployment was high in the Arab world, at around 25%, but this was not a new development and therefore cannot explain the timing of the protests. Similarly, the decline of public welfare functions and the rise of parallel networks of social welfare provision were not recent phenomena. The rollback of the state originated in the fiscal crises of the 1980s experienced across most countries in the region, particularly those with low per capita oil reserves.

In short, by 2011, on the eve of the revolts, there was no singular economic shock to point to as a candidate for igniting the uprisings. Subsidies were not being cut; unemployment, while high, was not rising; and growth rates and investment ratios were on the rise and at comfortable levels. Furthermore, as the literature on social movements argues, economic grievances at best provide incomplete explanations for mass mobilization (McAdam 1982).

Instead, as we argue later in this chapter, *discontent on the economic front interacted with a broader sociopolitical context to ignite the uprisings.* In particular, economic stagnation mixed with the *perceived* rise in inequalities and lack of "social justice," a perception that had been mounting as a result of the rollback of the state and economic liberalization characterized by cronyism. As a result, access to economic opportunities was not meritocratic or governed by a level playing field, but rather was mediated by connections to political leaders and their narrowing circles of allies. In the context of redistributive commitments by rulers to populations, which increased citizen expectations of the state in both the "populist" republics and the more conservative monarchies, the inability of government to provide for citizens and a growing sense of economic insecurity were particularly egregious. This combination of factors created a dam of accumulated grievances and rising aspirations, ready to burst. The interlinkages between economic and political grievances point to the value of a political economy perspective in understanding the Arab uprisings.

A brief application of these claims to the case of Tunisia, where the revolts began, helps to illustrate our logic. At first glance, Tunisia was the least likely country in the region to have ignited the Arab uprisings. Tunisia experienced steady growth rates in the previous decade and exceeded the regional average on a variety of social indicators, such as literacy, school enrollment, and life expectancy. Among the non-oil economies in the region, Tunisia had the most developed welfare state institutions, which helped to create a more robust middle class than was found in other Arab countries. The state also ran a variety of social assistance programs, and poverty rates were lower than in neighboring countries. In addition, until the late 1990s, business-government relations were less corrupt and capital was less concentrated than in other countries with similar industrial profiles. Politically, Tunisia also appeared to be an improbable place to set off the uprisings. The Tunisian state was notoriously repressive, leaving far less scope for civil society activism and public expression than in many other countries in the region. The ruling party had penetrated all aspects of civic and political life, a task facilitated by the country's small size. Although many Tunisians did not like Ben 'Ali, fear of unrest, as experienced in neighboring Algeria—which underwent a bloody civil war in the 1990s—seemed to reduce their appetite for regime change.

Paradoxically, Tunisia's socioeconomic achievements may be an important component of an explanation for the spread of mass mobilization against Ben 'Ali. Older generations of Tunisians had experienced genuine social mobility in their lifetimes, particularly during the first few decades after independence under Bourguiba's rule, and had developed high expectations of their state. Their children could no longer expect to advance socioeconomically, even with graduate degrees. Furthermore, the history of relatively minimal corruption in state-business relations made the concentration of economic opportunities in the hands of the Ben 'Ali and Trabelsi families all the more scandalous. In effect, under Ben 'Ali's rule, the authoritarian coalition gradually narrowed. By the time marginalized elements of society and Tunisians in neglected regions rose up against Ben 'Ali, the state's traditional sources of support— the middle classes and business interests—joined in the revolt again the ruler and his cronies (Kaboub 2012).

In the next section, we develop the elements of a more systematic account of the Arab uprisings.

Toward a Political Economy of the Arab Spring

A framework to explain the Arab uprisings should provide an account of the socioeconomic and political evolution of the Arab republics that would explain both the persistence of autocracy until 2011 and its eventual collapse and should do so in a way that is empirically verifiable. The next edition of this book will focus centrally on this challenge. Here we simply outline elements of the emerging picture. Different analysts would approach such an ambitious question in distinct ways. Some would stress contingency and agency, and undeniably, there were such elements in the particular timing of the uprisings in Tunisia and Egypt. But we contend here that there must also have been structural factors that opened up a window of opportunity from which the main protagonists in the uprisings profited.

What are the key elements of this framework? Our account begins with the rollback of the state and the decline of public services, which palpably increased insecurity among non-elite populations. With the fiscal crisis of the state and the adoption of market-oriented reforms, the social constituencies of authoritarian rulers gradually narrowed, and the class of privileged, well-connected elites who emerged profited from special access to economic opportunities. The rise of crony capitalism across the region reflected shifts in economic structures that led to the growing de facto exclusion of the middle classes from opportunities for socioeconomic advancement. Perhaps most important, cronyism and rising economic insecurity fueled perceptions of inequality and violations of norms of social justice. Later we develop each of the pieces of this story in more detail, including the rollback of the state, the shifting composition of the authoritarian coalition and the rise of crony capitalism, the perceived marginalization of the middle classes, and rising inequality. We then address the role of political Islam before, during, and after the revolts.

The Rollback of the State and
Deteriorating Economic Security

In the postcolonial period, the state played an unusually important role in economies across the Arab world. In this respect, Richards and Waterbury highlight parallels between the political economies of the Middle East and the socialist economies of the former Soviet bloc.

A leading family of structural narratives on the Arab uprisings focuses on a slow transition from quasi-socialism in which the rollback of the state, which began in the mid-1980s, ultimately led to the breakdown of the social contract underlying the autocratic bargain (Karshenas and Moghadam 2006; Yousef 2004b). Such accounts cannot claim that state rollback is the proximate cause of the revolts, given the long time lag. Nonetheless, to analyze the ultimate collapse of the system we need an understanding of why and how reforms were delayed, which mechanisms were used by autocrats to remain in power, even as market forces chipped away at their authority, and which contradictions emerged in this late autocratic "equilibrium" characterized by selective repression, co-optation, and cronyism. In this section, we briefly review the empirical record of state rollback and the related decline of public welfare functions.

A look at key economic performance indicators for the Arab developing countries as a group, from 1980 to 2008, depicted in Figure 16.1, shows clearly that the rollback of the state began twenty-five years ago.

Government expenditure shot up in the 1970s on the back of rising oil wealth in the region, but fell precipitously in the 1980s, reaching 22% of GDP in the early 1990s, a low figure by international standards. At the same time, private investment did not rise significantly to make up for the shortfall.

Economic reforms adopted in the 1980s in the Arab world tended to hurt the poor and middle classes disproportionately. For example, subsidies to agriculture were cut deeply, which was particularly damaging to the rural poor, while lower public-sector wages and hiring freezes hurt civil servants and formal-sector workers. Given the de facto importance of government employment in post-independence welfare regimes across the region, these reforms were especially damaging to the nascent middle classes. In countries across the region, including Egypt, Jordan, Morocco, and Tunisia, protests erupted. In particular, attempts to cut subsidies on basic

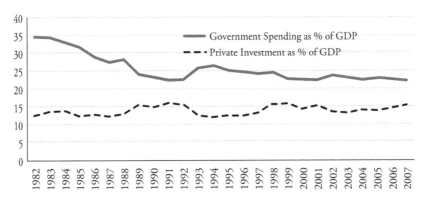

FIGURE 16.1   Government spending and private investment as a percentage of GDP for developing Arab countries, 1982–2007
SOURCE: World Bank, *World Development Indicators*, various years, averages for all developing Arab countries

food items sparked "bread riots," which often compelled rulers to retract agreements with international financial institutions to reduce these expenditures.

In the post-independence period, rulers across the region, in both the "populist" republics and the "conservative" monarchies, expanded the public welfare infrastructure as part of state- and nation-building processes. In some countries, citizens had constitutional guarantees to basic health care and education. The first few decades after independence witnessed major gains in quality-of-life indicators. For example, in 1960, the infant mortality rate (IMR) was slightly higher in Arab states (154 deaths per 1,000 births) than in sub-Saharan Africa (151 per 1,000). In 2011, the IMR in the Arab world was 30 per 1,000 births and in sub-Saharan Africa it was 86. Thus, over a forty-five-year period, the Arab states maintained the highest annualized rate of IMR reduction (3.6%), three times faster than in Africa (1.2%), one-third faster than in Asia (2.7%), and slightly faster than in Latin America (3.4%). In addition, poverty rates are significantly lower in the Middle East than in other regions of the Global South.[2] Thus, in the decades after independence, Arab citizens experienced important and tangible socioeconomic gains that arguably raised their aspirations for themselves and their children.

Access to basic services and stable employment provided a sense of economic security, while human development gains enabled earlier generations in post-independence Arab countries to enjoy some social mobility. Formal-sector workers have always enjoyed far more benefits and job security than the large portion of Arab populations who work in the informal sector.[3] Formal-sector workers, however, especially civil servants and members of the security forces, were important foundations of authoritarian bargains across the region and therefore were more politically consequential for incumbent rulers. As a result, any breakdown in the public welfare infrastructure that affected employees in the public sector was bound to be politically risky.

The steady decline in public welfare institutions since the 1980s has affected all segments of the population beyond the wealthy elite, but it has been particularly damaging for the poor, who rely on government services. As Figure 16.2 shows, the Middle East stands out in cross-regional comparative perspective for its high levels of government consumption as a percentage of GDP, which broadly measures the provision of government services.

Figure 16.2 demonstrates that government consumption as a percentage of GDP in the developing countries of the Middle East exceeded that of other global regions in the 1970s but, unlike all other regions, exhibited a downward trend. In the early 1980s, it first dipped below levels in OECD countries and decreased steadily thereafter, although it still exceeded that of other developing regions except sub-Saharan Africa until the late 1990s (World Bank, *World Development Indicators*, various years).

Government spending on health and education has remained steady or even increased in the past few decades.[4] Expenditures do not, however, provide a satisfactory account of how populations actually experience their welfare regimes, since funds can be spent inefficiently or misused (Esping-Andersen 1990; Mares 2003). More systematic research is needed to track the decline of public health and educational institutions, and the fourth edition of this book will provide detail on this important issue. In particular, it is vital to know more about the quality of the services provided

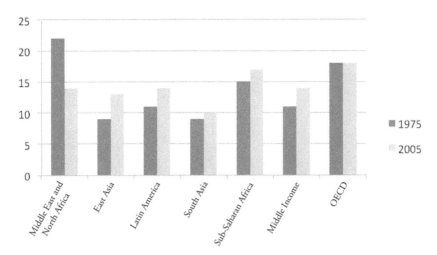

FIGURE 16.2   General government final consumption as a percentage of GDP, various global regions, 1975 and 2005
SOURCE: World Bank, *World Development Indicators*, 1975 and 2005, for all regions in the Global South, including developing countries only

and about the welfare infrastructure, medical and educational personnel, absenteeism, and other difficult-to-research yet core dimensions of welfare systems.

In the absence of information on the quality of social services, the breakdown of expenditures on health offers a preliminary picture of how citizens actually experience their health systems. Out-of-pocket spending as a percentage of total spending on health care is a useful indicator of economic insecurity because it tracks the degree to which households assume the burden of health coverage, which is particularly onerous for the poor. Figure 16.3 depicts levels of out-of-pocket spending on health in selected Arab countries and compares them to the regional average and to the average for middle-income countries.

Unfortunately, it is impossible to get an accurate picture of longer-term trends given data limitations. Nonetheless, the figure shows that, even since the mid-1990s, the burden of health expenses has increasingly fallen on the shoulders of households, particularly in Egypt. In Tunisia, which is known for its relatively developed public welfare programs, out-of-pocket spending on health exhibited a gradual increase in the past decade. Although the average level of household spending on health in Middle Eastern developing economies declined slightly from a peak in 2000, it still exceeded that of middle-income countries as a whole.

As noted, the rollback of the state and declining public welfare cannot provide a proximate explanation for the Arab uprisings, but economic deterioration raises the question of why populations did not rise up against their governments when the state was no longer holding up its side of the authoritarian bargain. In the 1980s and 1990s, economic crises in other regions, such as Latin America and sub-Saharan

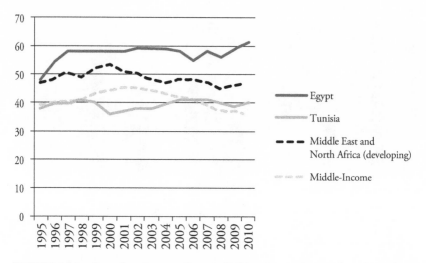

FIGURE 16.3   Out-of-pocket spending on health as a percentage of total spending on health in selected countries and regions, 1995–2010
SOURCE: WHO, *Health for All* database, various years

Africa, had helped to provoke regime change during the near-synchronous "third wave" of democratization (Huntington 1991). In the Middle East, however, autocratic rulers did not open up the political space in order to reduce social pressures stemming from the decline in economic resources. To the contrary, the opposite may have happened, as suggested by Figure 16.4, which depicts the evolution of political rights between 1980 and 2010.

In 2010, the region was politically less open than in the mid-1980s, with the average score of citizen empowerment for the region falling from about 6 in 1980 to 1.2 in 2010 on a scale from 0 to 14, with 0 depicting complete dictatorship.

Although economic factors are not sufficient causes for the downfall of dictatorship (Pepinsky 2009), it is worth investigating why economic crises were associated with democratization in other regions more than in the Middle East. The literature on authoritarian durability is voluminous.[5] External support for authoritarian rule is a distinctive feature of the region and therefore a key component of any explanation for the persistence of authoritarianism in the Middle East in comparison with other regions (El Badawi and Makdisi 2007; Bellin 2004; Levitsky and Way 2010). External support provided rents in the form of aid and military support but helped to fuel the militarization of the region, which in turn facilitated state repression of opposition groups.

Repression, Co-optation, and the Authoritarian Bargain

Repression is certainly a core component of any account of authoritarian persistence. The threat of harassment, persecution, imprisonment, torture, and death is a

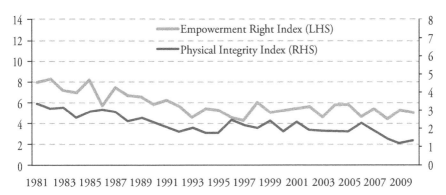

FIGURE 16.4   Repression and freedom indices, average for all Arab countries, 1981–2010
SOURCE: Cingranelli-Richards (CIRI), *Human Rights Dataset,* various years

powerful disincentive for anti-regime activism. The level of spending on security matters attests that repression had become an essential tool in the preservation of autocratic regimes in the late 1990s. Figure 16.4 depicts average levels of repression in the region as measured by the Index of Physical Integrity on a scale from 0 to 8 where 0 is maximum repression. Between 1980 and 2010, the average value of the index for the Arab countries fell from 4.5 to 2.9.

It is virtually a truism that repression is never a sufficient tool of political control, nor even the most effective. The literature on persistent authoritarianism in the Middle East has described in detail how (and in some cases why) different regimes chose to respond with distinctive mixes of co-optation and repression to maintain their control. Autocrats aimed to maximize their dwindling assets by dividing citizens into groups that benefited from cooperation while others were subject to repression and neglect. In Middle Eastern countries that lacked high per capita oil wealth, authoritarian rulers sought to strengthen their coalitions by co-opting the middle classes, which were largely composed of public-sector employees and some formal-sector workers.

Mass co-optation was achieved in large part through direct economic benefits in the form of subsidies for goods that were consumed relatively less by the poor, such as petroleum and energy. (Earlier subsidies for small-scale agriculture and for basic food items that benefited the poor had been reduced or eliminated.) A cross-regional comparison of petroleum subsidies reveals the specificity of the Middle East in this regard (see Figure 16.5).

Energy subsidies have grown over time, and by 2011 they were much higher in the Middle East and North Africa (MENA) than in any other region of the world. In absolute terms, about 50% of global energy subsidies are disbursed in the MENA region. These subsidies represent about 8.5% of regional GDP and 22% of total government revenues, which is much larger than in other developing regions; subsidies tend to be negligible in the advanced economies. Within the region, levels of subsidies vary, but twelve of the twenty countries in the region have subsidies above 5% of GDP.

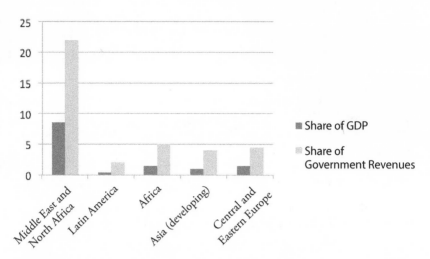

FIGURE 16.5   Energy subsidies as a share of GDP and government revenues in various regions, 2011
SOURCE: International Monetary Fund (2013)

About half of all subsidies in the Middle East go to petroleum products, followed by electricity. Government expenditures on these subsidies have gone up in recent years, together with energy prices. In many countries, they now represent an expense several times higher than total spending on health or on education.[6] This phenomenon is not restricted to oil exporters. For example, in 2011, energy subsidies represented 41% of government revenues in Egypt, 24% in Yemen, 22% in Jordan, and 19% in Lebanon, in contrast with "only" 10% in Kuwait, 15% in the United Arab Emirates, and 18% in Saudi Arabia. Among oil producers, Algeria and Iran had particularly large energy subsidies—27% and 50% of their respective revenues—even *after* the famous Iranian subsidy reforms.

It is well known that such subsidies are very regressive, as oil products tend to be consumed in much larger quantities by richer people. For example, a study in Egypt shows that in the case of oil petroleum subsidies, 46% of the benefits accrued to the top quintile in 2008 (Abouleinem, Al-Tathy, and Kheir-el-Din 2009). Once in place, it is almost impossible to reduce or eliminate subsidies because of the threat of political backlash by key constituents.

The large share of subsidies in the budgets of Arab governments exacerbated economic crises and furthered the decline of public services. Subsidies consumed ever-larger portions of government budgets, leaving less for investment in public services. Over time the effort to co-opt key societal groups through the extension and continuation of subsidies backfired by undermining social services and other public programs that citizens had come to expect and by limiting public investment, especially in rural and disadvantaged areas.

At the same time, fiscal regimes seem to have become more pro-rich over time. Tax rates have been relatively low, particularly in the countries with large hydrocarbon reserves. Even in the countries with low per capita natural resources, direct taxes now constitute a relatively small share of fiscal receipts. Indirect taxes, which are inherently regressive because they are applied to consumers across the board, regardless of income level (Imam and Jacobs 2007), became a more important component of tax revenue in these countries after the reforms of the 1990s.

In the mix of co-optation and repression—or carrots and sticks—changes in the former mattered more in explaining authoritarian breakdown than the latter. (Co-optation was probably more consequential for authoritarian durability too, but that is beyond the scope of this analysis.) If repression helped authoritarian regimes to endure, it cannot explain why dictatorships collapsed across the region: repression was constant, and had even been increasing since the 1990s (as seen in Figure 16.4), but rulers in multiple Arab countries were overthrown. Thus, any explanation for authoritarian breakdown must probe the evolution of co-optation. In the next section, we trace the narrowing of authoritarian social coalitions—that is, the groups that were favored in domestic political economies—and describe how this factor contributed to authoritarian breakdown.

Crony Capitalism

By the mid-1990s, the old social contract in post-independence Arab countries was already dead but had not been replaced by a new successful model. Over time alliances between autocrats and elite capital were increasingly consolidated. In this section, we describe the rise of crony capitalism, a central feature of authoritarian coalitions in the Arab countries. In the next edition of this book, the political economy of crony capitalism will be developed more fully.

The popular discontent that led to the uprisings can be traced to two main elements of economic policy: the rollback of the state and the consolidation of close relations between the state and particular elements of the business elite under economic liberalism. The central question of why the Arab region underperformed in terms of job creation, given what looked on paper to be impeccable market reforms, has been debated for years. Some have argued that the market reforms did not go far enough (Noland and Pack 2007; World Bank 2009), while others hold that economics became dominated by networks of privilege (Heydemann 2004) or even crony capitalists (Saadowski 1991) with myopic short-term interests that stifled competition, innovation, and ultimately job creation.

Conceptually, there is nothing intrinsically bad about close state-business relations. The case of South Korean *chaebols* illustrates how industrial policy can foster accumulation and the development of new sectors, even when state-business relations are characterized by cronyism (Kang 2002; Khan 2010). To the extent that they provide the right incentives to perform, close state-business relations can form the basis for dynamic capitalism. Under different circumstances and with less effective states, tight state-business relations can also become sources of undue influence, corruption, and other forms of rent-seeking that distort economic and political incentives. In the Arab world, however, particularly in the non-oil-exporting countries, crony capitalism did not appear to drive inclusive growth or development.

Popular perceptions of business elites have become quite negative in the region. Cronyism is now seen as both the key characteristic of the economic opening that started in the 1990s and accelerated in the 2000s and the source of many ills, including the job deficit, the rise in inequalities, and the perpetuation of authoritarian rule. The perceived "corruption" of the political and business elites was a key driving force of popular discontent. For example, a Pew survey reveals that in 2010 corruption was the top concern of Egyptians, with 46% listing it as their main concern even ahead of lack of democracy and poor economic conditions (Pew Research Center Report 2011). Changes in the corruption ratings of Arab countries in the Transparency International Index confirm popular perception: for example, in 2005, Egypt ranked 70th, Tunisia ranked 43rd, Libya ranked 117th, and Yemen ranked 103rd out of 158 rankings on the Corruption Perceptions Index (CPI). Perceived corruption increased markedly in the following three years. In 2008, Egypt dropped to 115th, Tunisia to 62nd, Libya to 126th, and Yemen to 141st out of 180 rankings on the CPI.

We now know that this was not just about perceptions. In both Tunisia and Egypt, the ongoing trials of leading businessmen are starting to shed light on the ways in which influence was yielded for private gain. Cronyism entailed practices such as the granting of monopoly rights to close associates of the rulers, the selling of public firms and land at reduced prices, and the manipulation of the financial markets for the benefits of a few insiders. In Tunisia, the Ben 'Ali and Trabelsi families monopolized business opportunities and even expropriated the real estate and business holdings of wealthy elites. In this relatively small country, stories of Ben 'Ali and Trabelsi were an open secret. Anonymous Samizdat tracts circulated freely, with titles such as "Les Sept Familles Qui Pillent la Tunisie" ("The Seven Families Who Are Pillaging Tunisia") appearing mysteriously in mailboxes in greater Tunis during the late 1990s and 2000s. The observations of American diplomats, revealed in cables released by Wikileaks, echoed and provided further details on the extent of corruption around the presidential palace in Tunis. Similar stories about favoritism and insiders abound in Syria, Libya, Yemen, and Algeria, where political cronies seem to control large chunks of the private sector (Alley 2010; Dillman 2000; Haddad 2012; Tlemcani 1999; Vandewalle 1998).

In Egypt, the trend accelerated in the last decade with the "businessmen" cabinet headed by Ahmad Nazif (2004–2011). Two iconic cases under investigation now illustrate the nature of privileges. The first is that of Ezz Steel, whose head has been sentenced by an Egyptian court on multiple charges of corruption. Ahmad Ezz, a very successful businessman who dominated the steel industry after 2000, is now accused of having lobbied on behalf of his firm on issues related to raising external tariffs, increasing protection in the steel sector, and relaxing anti-monopoly constraints. A prominent member of the National Democratic Party (NDP), the dominant party in the Egyptian political system, Ezz was extremely well connected. He held influential positions such as MP and chair of the Budget Committee in Parliament, which among other things oversees the work of the Competition Commission and trade policy; member of the NDP's influential Policy Committee, which was chaired by Gamal Mubarak; and NDP secretary for organizational affairs. A second example, also the focus of several current court cases, is that of Palm Hill Corporation, the second-largest real estate developer in Egypt. The main owner of Palm Hill, Ahmed El-Maghrabi, was minister of housing in the Nazif cabinet and has been accused of exploiting his ministerial position to sell the company large tracts of land in various parts of the country at exceptionally cheap prices, giving his firm a big advantage over competitors (Ahram Online 2011). In Tunisia, the case of Orange Tunisie, the local affiliate of a French telecommunications company, is widely cited. In 2009, Investec, a company held by Marwan Mabrouk and his wife, Cyrine Ben 'Ali, a daughter of the deposed dictator, won a bid for the third mobile phone network in Tunisia. (The two finalists in the call for bids were both sons-in-law of the president.) After gaining the telephone network, Mabrouk was named president of the board of Orange Tunisie and obtained interest-free bank loans from institutions linked to the state. The company is now under investigation, and the Tunisian state holds 51% of its shares (Beaugé 2011).

The precise nature of state-business relations varied from country to country, with important ramifications for the dynamics of authoritarian stability and breakdown. For example, in the aftermath of the uprising the importance of the military in the Egyptian domestic economy became well known, albeit in imprecise terms. The important stakes of military institutions and high-ranking officers in protected industries help to explain why the Supreme Council of the Armed Forces (SCAF), a key backbone of the authoritarian regime, allowed Mubarak to fall but stymied substantive democratization in post-Mubarak Egypt (Marshall and Stacher 2012). Without an understanding of the military's role in the domestic political economy, it is impossible to understand political developments during and after the uprisings. In Tunisia, the military was far less central in the authoritarian coalition, which in part accounts for General Rachid Ammar's unwillingness to shoot protesters, a key juncture in the overthrow of Ben 'Ali. Furthermore, the elite coalition in Ben 'Ali's regime appeared to have narrowed much more than in Egypt, although this hypothesis deserves more systematic analysis. As a result, by the time mass protests erupted against the Ben 'Ali regime, many Tunisian capitalists who were not integrated into his networks of privilege accepted his downfall. In Egypt, Gamal Mubarak and his allies had gained important footholds in the Egyptian economy and profited from lucrative international deals, but this faction of the regime was counterbalanced by a strong and historically powerful protectionist bourgeoisie, which included but was not limited to the military.

The literature on contemporary Arab capitalism is still in its infancy. Some work analyzes state-business relations in the period prior to the uprisings in Egypt (Kienle 2001; Roll 2010; Sfakianakis 2004), Morocco (Cammett 2007; Catusse 2008; Henry 1996), Syria (Haddad 2012; Kienle 2002), Tunisia (Bellin 2002; Cammett 2007; Hibou 2006), and the Gulf (Chaudhry 1997; Hertog 2010; Moore 2004; Vitalis 2007), as well as the region as a whole (Heydemann 2004; Schlumberger 2007). With few, if any, direct measurements of the extent of favoritism, however, there have been no serious attempts to statistically evaluate the socioeconomic impact of cronyism.

A recent study of the Egyptian stock market around the momentous events of 2010 sheds some light on these issues. In evaluating the value of firms' political connections through an event study of stock market reaction to the revolution, Hamouda Chekir and Ishac Diwan (2012) estimate these to be about 20% of the firms' value.

They also compare the past corporate performance of connected and unconnected firms. In 2002, connected firms were about the same size as the other firms on the exchange, but by 2010 their median size had increased to seven times the median of nonconnected firms, which had barely grown. Their analyses indicate that connected firms had a larger market share than their nonconnected competitors and borrowed much more than their competitors, on more favorable terms. (By 2010, the top twenty connected firms received 80% of the credit going to the largest one hundred Egyptian firms.) Importantly, they also found that the connected firms were less profitable than the nonconnected firms. At a minimum, even if favors were intended as industrial policy measures, they were not particularly successful. More likely, they were run inefficiently by regime cronies who had been appointed because they were trusted rather than skilled, in part to deny the heights of the economy to potential regime opponents. Another possibility is that they directed their profits to bankrolling the ruling party and to themselves. Indeed, well-connected businessmen became very rich and are central to the perception of a large rise in the 1% in Egypt in recent years. This arrangement then channeled capital flows to relatively inefficient sectors, reducing economic growth directly, while starving small and medium-size enterprises for credit, despite the fact that they provided a disproportionate share of new jobs (Assaad 2009). Moreover, this unfair competition may have reduced the dynamism of the economy as a whole. The key question is whether a dynamic form of capitalism was emerging or whether the economy was stuck in a low investment trap. That private investment in Egypt never went beyond 15% of GDP, with large capital flight (Kar and Curcio 2011) and in conjunction with the stagnation of unconnected firms, militates for the second interpretation.

Close state-business relations in the context of underperforming economies across the Arab world highlight a puzzle about the region: Why was cronyism bad for growth in Arab countries but not necessarily in other regions? How did it affect economic growth and development in the region and how, in turn, did this play into uprisings? To address these questions, it is essential to provide systematic data on the characteristics of the *ancien régime* and to develop a clearer sense of the impact of cronyism on economic performance and, more generally, on the legitimacy of authoritarian regimes. This suggests three main areas for research on state-business relations in the Arab world: Is there systematic evidence of favoritism? How did the connected firms operate in an economy that was ostensibly liberalized and theoretically less subject to government regulation? Are there objective ways of evaluating the impact on economic and political performance of the types of state-business relations that developed in the 2000s in the region?

More work remains to be done on Arab capitalism, but at a minimum, it is clear that cronyism is a fundamental building block in a political economy account of the uprisings. Crony capitalism arguably contributed to the revolts through at least two channels. First, as we have suggested, it may be an important factor behind economic underperformance in the region. As we argue in the next two sections, cronyism signaled the narrowing of authoritarian coalitions, squeezed out the middle classes, a key constituency of post-independence Arab regimes, and fueled perceptions of rising inequality.

The Evolution of the Authoritarian Coalition
and the Role of the Middle Classes

In the initial decades after independence, Arab governments—and especially the republics—introduced policies that led to significant social change. In particular, statist economic policies coupled with welfare programs and subsidies on basic food items and fuel facilitated the rise of proto-middle classes. Public-sector workers, benefiting from job security and social benefits, were the most important component of the new middle classes. Also emerging was a professional class composed of doctors, lawyers, engineers, and others who enjoyed enhanced social status and a decent standard of living.

The middle classes appear to be a central actor of change in the Arab republics. For decades, Arab autocrats had placed a premium on retaining the mainly secular, middle-class-led parties and factions, either within the authoritarian coalition or as part of the legal opposition. For the republics in particular, secular and liberal ideologies were at the center of their Arab nationalist foundations (Browers 2009). In the 1950s, leaders such as Bourguiba and Nasser adopted an Atatürkian model of modernization in which the middle classes played a legitimizing role. Thus, for Arab autocrats, losing their middle-class anchors was tantamount to becoming naked dictatorships with no operational narrative.

There are indications that the middle classes have been hurt by the economic liberalization programs of the 1990s, and especially by their acceleration in the 2000s. Apart from the direct effects on the labor market, the interests of the middle classes have been threatened in many ways by the rollback of the state and the rise of neoliberalism.[7] In addition, low public-sector wages fueled petty corruption in areas such as health and education, generating another important source of discontent. To be sure, governments retained important policies aiding the middle classes, such as subsidies on food and fuel; given policy lock-in and the threat of political backlash from a key constituency in regime coalitions, it was difficult for governments to eliminate subsidies. As a result, the authoritarian bargain of the past decade evolved into an alliance between elite capital and elements of the middle classes that delivered economic benefits to coalition members, partly in the form of subsidies, but was less and less supportive of non-elite elements.

Further research is needed to understand more clearly the changing real and perceived socioeconomic conditions of the middle classes. Data from the World Values Survey provide a preliminary indication of shifting self-perceptions of citizens in Egypt. The survey, which asks respondents to identify the class to which they belong, provides a broad, self-assessed measure of well-being that goes well beyond income in capturing lifelong income, aspirations, and ownership of assets. A comparison of data from 2000 and 2008 indicates that the size of the middle classes has shrunk from 65 to 58% of the population in favor of the poor.[8]

Beyond its relative size, the nature of the middle classes has changed over time. Until recently, specialists did not seem to believe that the middle classes could play an active role in leading political change (for example, see Bellin 2002; Cammett 2007). With the middle classes incorporated into the system as civil servants and employees of state-owned enterprises, their influence on policy formulation and their ability to play the role of an "autonomous actor" were effectively undercut. A new, market-oriented middle class rose in the late 1990s in response to economic liberalization. The newcomers tended to be small merchants and industrialists, often in the informal sector, who benefited from the pro-market reforms, as well as the small but expanding skilled component of the formal private-sector labor market. This group has been more politically active than older elements of the private sector (Nasr 2009). For example, the new, pro-market middle class played an important role in securing the success of the Iranian revolution in 1979 and the rise of the Justice and Development party (AKP) in Turkey, and it has become a more vocal and assertive element in the Moroccan business community (Cammett 2007; Catusse 2008; Demiralp 2009; Gumuscu and Sert 2009).

A comparative analysis of opinion polls in Egypt shows that the middle class dramatically increased its support for democracy between 2000 and 2008, and that this was accompanied by a large rise in perceptions of inequality (Diwan 2013). While the youth may have mobilized more than other age groups in protests across the Arab region, these surveys do not support the claim that their views differ from those of their parents on the desirability of democracy at the present juncture.[9] To the extent that the underlying forces driving public opinion are connected to the unemployment of skilled youth, a major phenomenon for the middle classes, it seems that the parents of Egyptian middle-class youth became as unhappy as their children about the lack of job opportunities and were thus compelled to favor regime change and democracy.

Deteriorating socioeconomic conditions combined with high aspirations increased discontent among the middle classes. As a result, they gradually withdrew their support for authoritarian regimes. Dissatisfaction with the status quo, however, cannot simply be inferred from real economic conditions. Perceived conditions are more important in translating grievances into action than objective economic indicators. To understand the unraveling of authoritarian coalitions, we must comprehend how the middle classes interpreted changing socioeconomic conditions in their societies. The next section addresses this component of our framework.

Perceived Inequality

The Arab region is not distinguished by exceptionally high levels of inequality, nor has inequality risen sharply (Bibi and Nabli 2011). Thus, rising absolute levels of inequality, as measured by household expenditures surveys, do not provide satisfactory explanations for the Arab uprisings. Rather, we argue that perceptions of inequality, which are refracted through particular sociopolitical contexts and reflect developments that are hard to measure, are critical to an account of authoritarian breakdown and social protest in the Arab countries.

It is tempting to make inequality a core driver of an understanding of the Arab Spring in the context of the transition from state quasi-socialism and populism toward capitalism. The equilibrium of the last decade is commonly described as a regime of crony and unequal capitalism. This system appears to have generated socially unacceptable inequalities, directly by supporting the growth of a class of the super-rich and indirectly by its inability to create sufficient good jobs for the newly educated middle classes. Yet no direct evidence suggests that inequality has risen sharply in the recent past. Household surveys reveal that consumption inequality (as measured by Gini coefficients) has risen moderately in Egypt, from about 0.3 in the 1990s to 0.35 in the 2000s (Belhaj and Wissa 2011; Bibi and Nabli 2011). In Tunisia, inequality as measured by consumption inequality fell, from about 0.43 in the mid-1980s to 0.39 in the mid-2000s, but there are also indications of a rise in the urban-rural divide. Furthermore, levels of inequality vary across the Arab transitioning countries, with lower levels in Egypt and higher levels in Tunisia (Bibi and Nabli 2011, 31).

There are two reasons to think that these statistics describe only a limited part of reality. First, household surveys are notorious for undercounting the rich. There are many indications of a rise in the income share of the 10% richest in society, who are perceived to have benefited most from a more market-oriented economy, and of the top 1%, who have benefited most from the rampant crony capitalism of the last decade. By some estimates, the top 10% in Egypt, Morocco, Jordan, and Syria may have commanded 30 to 40% of GDP by 2010.[10]

Second, grievances are also likely to be connected to changes in the *inequality of opportunities* rather than to only the inequality of incomes per se. Over time the rollback of the state had reduced the role of the state as an employer. In Egypt, for example, only 25% of the labor force worked for the state by 2009, declining from a height of 40% of the workers. In Jordan, the private sector has generated more jobs than in the past, but these jobs generally lack social insurance and/or are based on temporary or no contracts. Furthermore, the bifurcation between the formal and informal private sectors has sharpened. Informal-sector workers tend not to transition into formal-sector jobs, and although public-sector employment has increased in recent years, workers who previously held positions in the formal private sector are far more likely than informal-sector workers to move into government jobs (Assaad 2011). Recent studies show clearly that the large waves of more educated workers[11] entering the labor market were faced with an increasingly unfair situation whereby personal connections (*wasta*) and status were more important than diplomas in getting good jobs.[12] With shrinking government employment, these new entrants had to divide themselves between the formal private sector, which did not grow in proportional terms and where wages were higher than in the public sector, and a large and growing informal sector, where wages were lower than in the public sector (Assaad 2009). Furthermore, the decline of health and education systems, key drivers of social mobility, had limited the ability of non-elites to advance (Belhaj and Wissa 2011; Salehi-Isfahani, Belhaj, and Assaad 2011). Empirical research has only recently started to focus on this type of inequality, but recent work is starting to show that unlike simple consumption-based measures, such as the Gini coefficient, measures of inequality of opportunity show a dramatic increase in recent years.

To summarize, inequality based on standard consumption-based measures does not appear to be a driver of the uprisings. There is no evidence of a sharp spike in this type of inequality in the Arab countries; levels of inequality varied across the countries that witnessed mass protests, and the region as a whole does not exhibit particularly high levels of income inequality. Recent analyses, however, indicate that inequalities of opportunity were on the rise across the non-oil-exporting countries of the region. In the context of post-independence social bargains, in which citizens experienced and came to expect real social mobility as a result of state economic and welfare policies, the inability to advance socioeconomically may have been especially frustrating. Before we bring together the full narrative of our framework, it is essential to address one additional factor—the role of political Islam—in the evolution of politics across the region both prior to and during the uprisings.

The Role of Political Islam in the Arab Uprisings

In the aftermath of the Arab uprisings, Islamists have become increasingly important if not dominant actors in Tunisia and Egypt and, to a lesser degree, in Libya and Yemen. It is widely accepted that the uprisings were not driven by Islamists, or even by increased popular support for Islamists, who were the most vocal opponents of authoritarian rulers. Rather, Islamists were the main beneficiaries of the transitional political systems that emerged after dictators were ousted.

Although Islamists did not initiate or lead the revolts, they may have played an indirect role in driving the Arab uprisings.[13] In particular, two mechanisms related to political Islam may have contributed to the defection of the middle classes from authoritarian bargains. First, since the 1990s, Islamists across the region have become less threatening because they have increasingly moderated their ideology and tactics. For example, in 2004 the Muslim Brotherhood in Egypt made a public commitment to abide by a constitutional and democratic system that called for the recognition of "the people as the source of all authority," and it endorsed the principles of the transfer of power through free elections, the freedom of belief and expression, the freedom to form political parties, and the independence of the judiciary (Shahin 2005).[14] The moderation of Islamists may have altered the calculations of socially liberal groups that had feared a takeover by Islamic parties because of their divergent views on issues such as civil rights, the separation of mosque and state, the role of women in society, and foreign policy. Even in the context of declining economic benefits, middle-class elements may have opted to support autocrats as long as Islamists championed a very different picture of civic and political life. As more moderate Islamic parties emerged, they may have garnered more support or at least tolerance among the middle classes.[15]At the same time, insurgent groups using violent tactics declined. If fear of Islamism had perpetuated authoritarian rule (Lust 2011), then declining fear of Islamism undercut support for dictators.

Second, some of the messages of Islamist parties, which emphasized corruption and the lack of social justice under authoritarian rulers, reflected and may even have amplified growing discontent among the middle classes. Indeed, the leaders and cadres of mainstream Islamist groups, such as the Muslim Brotherhood in Egypt and its branches and analogous organizations in other Arab countries, were composed of middle-class professionals who were shut out of employment and other opportunities under crony capitalist systems (Burgat 2003; Esposito 1997; Fuller 2004). Islamism does not offer a clear-cut and uniform ideology on the market. Islamic thinkers and groups disagree on the extent to which the teachings of Islam call for redistributive measures. A dominant ideological strain associated with the rise of moderate Islamist parties such as the AKP or the Muslim Brotherhood in Egypt and Al-Nahda in Tunisia, however, is congruent with middle-class redistributive goals and supportive of market-based systems.

Public opinion data indicate that support for democratization increased among the middle classes during the 2000s, including among proponents of Islamism. Opinion polls in the Arab world undertaken by the Arab Barometer reveal that rising demand for democracy is positively correlated with support for political Islam: people favor more democracy and more Islamism at the same time. A more detailed analysis using data from the World Values Survey for Egypt shows that adherents of Islamism did not support democracy as much as secularists in 2000. By 2008, the same pattern held, except that middle-class supporters of Islamism had become, like secularists, a force for democratization (Diwan 2013). This finding suggests that Islamism acts as a conservative veil for the poor only, trumping their class interests. After 2008, however, this effect did not operate among the middle classes, either because they were better educated and/or because they were more likely to be influenced by more moderate parties within the Islamist umbrella. This supports and refines Mark Tessler's (2011) argument that support for political Islam is congruent with rising support for democracy and also shows that this claim applies to the middle classes but not the poor.

Islamists were not central actors in the uprisings that toppled authoritarian rulers, but their role in society and politics may have contributed to the defection of the middle classes from authoritarian coalitions, a key step in the breakdown of authoritarian rule. First, the declining fear of political Islam that accompanied the growing moderation of Islamist groups may have compelled secularists to distance themselves from autocratic rulers. Second, the messages of the Islamist opposition may have resonated with the middle classes, who viewed corruption and cronyism as obstacles to their social advancement.

In the next section, we combine the diverse factors addressed in this section to present a framework for understanding the Arab uprisings.

An Emerging Framework

The framework that emerges from this rapid exploration connects patterns of economic development (especially a shift toward a more market-based system, the decline of public welfare functions, and the rise of crony capitalism), social change (the rise in popular aspirations and grievances), and political change (the defection of the middle classes from the authoritarian coalition). This combination of changing economic circumstances and the attendant increase in inequality of opportunities fueled a spike in perceived inequality, which helped to unravel the implicit bargain between authoritarian rulers and key constituents.

To recap, this framework includes the following key elements. First, in the mid-1980s, the rollback of the state began without a concomitant democratic opening. In this context, an elite, capitalistic class benefited from personal connections to acquire disproportionate access to lucrative opportunities. The super-elite allied with state security apparatuses, which enforced their dominance through repression (sticks) and economic co-optation (carrots) to maintain the support of the middle class. Tight state-business relations within a supposedly "liberal" economic environment and political repression did not translate into a successful industrial policy. Instead, a system of gift exchange between the state and key constituents developed; the moderate performance of this system inhibited growth and thus did not foster the creation of good jobs. Across the Arab world, countries that initially adopted distinct economic strategies and political regimes ended up with variants of the same crony capitalist systems. Divide-and-rule strategies, based on a combination of blanket subsidies and repression as well as fearmongering about political Islam, were the foundation of an increasingly fragile governing coalition.

Supported by the West, this autocratic, low equilibrium lasted for several decades. For a time, with the co-optation of the middle classes through subsidies and fear of a takeover by Islamists, and with the poor repressed and struggling to make ends meet, authoritarianism could endure. Mounting fiscal pressures, driven in large part by rising subsidies and lower tax revenues, led to deteriorating social services and lower public investment, further hurting the poor and marginalized regions and leading populations to identify increasingly with the poor rather than the middle classes. In this context, middle-class elements defected from authoritarian coalitions and evolved into champions of change, driven by the lack of opportunities for socioeconomic advancement and anger about rising perceived inequalities.

THE DIFFICULTIES AHEAD:
POLITICS AND ECONOMIC REFORM
DURING TRANSITIONS

The Arab uprisings were a defining moment, a big celebration of life and creativity, reflecting a deep love of country. The protests engaged women as well as men, the young and the old, and members of all social classes. Mass mobilization in the face of repression revealed the bravery and sense of empowerment of the protesters, while the use of communications technologies highlighted the ingenuity and creativity of the youth. These moments will be remembered with affection and will enter historical founding myths. Clearly, they mark the end of the authoritarian state, even if its vestiges remain.

Revolutions tend to be protracted and messy. Economic factors often contribute to the outbreak of revolts in the first place, but once set in motion, revolutionary political change can aggravate and create new economic problems. Political uncertainty, a common feature of transitional moments, exacerbates economic crises. New institutions can take years to establish, and the simultaneous adoption of political and economic reforms is notoriously difficult.

The Arab transitional countries are entering this new era with a triple crisis—of the state, of capitalism, and even of national identity. The transitions are playing out against the backdrop of high expectations by the poor and an educated but often unemployed or underemployed middle class. In most of these countries, the economy requires serious restructuring and the state needs a major overhaul, but the attention of political leaders is presently focused elsewhere—largely on the role of Islam in politics and society. The price to pay for past sins seems enormous and carries over not just to economic technocratic issues but also to the necessity of coalition-building and long-term institutional reform. We briefly review the nature of the political and economic challenges facing the Middle East and discuss their implications for policymaking at the present juncture.

Political Developments After the Uprisings

Even where rulers have been deposed, genuine regime change remains in doubt in the Arab world. In Egypt, Mubarak was removed from power, but elements of his authoritarian coalition remain entrenched. The army retains significant privileges, despite the forced retirement of its top leaders, such as General Mohamed Hussein Tantawi. Although a new constitution was adopted and several rounds of elections were held, the process of political reform has been contested in Egypt, with opposition groups across the ideological spectrum claiming that they were marginalized and threatening to boycott elections. The process of writing the new constitution was rushed and fraught with tensions, with an Islamist-dominated body hastily writing and approving the draft while their opponents claimed they were sidelined from the process. In Yemen, the new president's cabinet and elements of the security forces retain many loyalists of the former president. In Libya, a sharp break took place in terms of both the identities of the new political leaders and the system of rule. Mu'ammar Qaddhafi was ousted, and the members of his family and close advisers are either under arrest or indicted in absentia. Nonetheless, the outcome of the revolution remains uncertain. Government authority is tenuous, and armed militias control much of the territory.

Of all the Arab countries where the protests successfully deposed dictators, Tunisia initially made the most progress toward the establishment of a new democratic system. In October 2011, elections for a constitutional assembly were held, ushering in a coalition government dominated by the main Islamist party, Al-Nahda, in alliance with secular parties. The process of writing the constitution has been more inclusive than in Egypt, with multiple drafts subject to public debate and input from diverse civil society groups. Yet politics have become increasingly polarized, particularly across the Islamist-secularist divide. Tensions have emerged over constitutional articles on the status of women and the role of religion in the constitution. Opposition groups claim that Al-Nahda has overplayed its hand by abandoning an inclusive process of political change and allying itself with, or at least tolerating, more extremist Islamist elements, which have perpetrated acts of violence with alarming frequency. As a result, further progress on political reform and efforts to tackle Tunisia's formidable economic problems are stalled.

The electoral victories of political Islam in the Arab transitioning countries were to be expected, given that Islamist parties were more organized early in the process and appeared to have deeper grassroots support. Even in Tunisia, where Islamists were brutally suppressed and virtually wiped out under Ben 'Ali's rule, Al-Nahda managed to maintain a subterranean base of supporters and quickly reactivated and expanded its local networks after its leadership returned to the country. Yet the grab for power by Islamists was surprising. In Egypt, the Muslim Brotherhood sought and won the presidency, despite earlier commitments to moderate its control over government institutions. In Tunisia, Al-Nahda became less and less willing to compromise with secular opponents once it secured the lion's share of the vote (although not the support of the majority of Tunisia when accounting for voter turnout and the inflationary effects of electoral rules on the distribution of seats).

Efforts by Islamists to monopolize power made sense in the short term, given that political domination in this critical historical moment would enable them to mold new political institutions in their favor. Moreover, the leadership of previously banned or heavily repressed Islamist groups feared that former regime elements as well as their secular opponents would deprive them of their "rightful" victories, if given the chance. In retrospect, however, Islamist domination of the political arena was probably a mistake. In light of the deterioration of political, security, and economic outcomes and the huge obstacles to delivering tangible improvements to people's lives, Islamists may face a serious drop in popular support. Mainstream Islamists, who had developed a reputation for "moderation" in the past decade, now also face the challenge of being outbid by other, more orthodox or extremist Islamist groups. Political liberalization has facilitated the rise of "Salafists," a diverse and heterogeneous category that threatens to chip away at the bases of more moderate Islamists. In response, groups such as Al-Nahda in Tunisia and the Muslim Brotherhood in Egypt are compelled to cater to more extremist constituencies and are becoming increasingly factionalized and splintered in the process. At the same time, mainstream Islamist groups, whose constituencies were based in the middle classes under authoritarian rule, are obliged to answer to a wider swath of society. For the first time, political Islam is being put to the test.

Divisions between Islamists and secularists reflect real tensions in society. In more consolidated democracies, political institutions should be able to manage these differences, addressing distributional and ideological conflict alike. In the context of institutional flux, in which new rules of the game need to be written and adopted, it is far more difficult to handle such tensions. Without capable leaders willing to compromise across ideological divides, polarization is the inevitable result. In the Arab transitioning countries, liberal elements have been pushed to reconstitute their ranks rapidly by radicalizing and mobilizing their supporters, focusing more on winning upcoming elections and blocking Islamist initiatives than on achieving good economic performance. For their part, Islamists have viewed the resort to street politics by liberal, secular groups as a nondemocratic rejection of their legitimate electoral gains. Their heightened sense of unfairness adds to a spiral of conflict that has ratcheted up tensions, making compromise all the more difficult. Ideally, upcoming parliamentary elections will reduce the cycle of polarization as coalitions are formed to craft social and economic programs, but whether inclusive elections can take place is uncertain under present circumstances.

At the minimum, it is now clear that transitions will take longer than expected. In the meantime, paralysis has taken hold, blocking decision-making by governing bodies. Moreover, the current environment, in which protracted insecurity, food shortages, and even economic collapse are real possibilities, invites the prospect of coups and military takeovers. The formation of a new political order has proved to be the greatest challenge in the Arab transitioning countries, bedeviling efforts to address the region's serious economic challenges.

Economic Challenges After the Uprisings

The revolutions were experienced as a negative economic shock. Tourism took a hit, capital flight accelerated, exports declined, and investment collapsed in Tunisia, Egypt, and Yemen. As a result, economic growth declined sharply in 2011—it was negative in Tunisia (–2%) and Yemen (–1%) and low in Egypt (1.8%) and Bahrain (2.1%). Output collapsed in Libya, given the disruption to its oil production (–60%). Across the region, unemployment increased.

Syria has been devastated. The human toll in death and suffering is staggering. Millions have been made refugees, in their country and in neighboring countries. Economic production has taken a big hit, and the destruction of assets is already estimated in the tens of billions of dollars. The economies of Lebanon and Jordan have also been negatively affected by regional instability and the influx of refugees.

Initially, governments reacted with expansionary policies to smooth out the downturn, especially in the face of rising social demands and the high expectations generated by the uprisings. Public-sector wages, subsidies, and government investment were increased in many countries around the region. In the Gulf countries, budgets were massively expanded. For example, expenditure increased by over one-third in Saudi Arabia. In the oil-importing countries, both external accounts and budget balances deteriorated. By 2012, fiscal deficits in Morocco, Jordan, Tunisia, and Lebanon had shot up to between 6 and 7% of GDP. In Egypt, the fiscal deficit ballooned at 12% of GDP, and international reserves plummeted.

As a result of these developments, by 2012 governments in oil-importing countries had no fiscal space to continue with stimulus programs, and therefore growth remained low in 2012 (about 2 to 3%). Expansionary policies were supported mainly by domestic debt levels as aid did not rise, despite repeated promises.[16] Unlike other regions that have undergone economic and political transitions simultaneously, notably eastern Europe, no external actor has eased the transition with large-scale aid and promises of a future economic and political union. Indeed, the uprisings occurred in the context of a global economic downturn and the Eurozone crisis, which has restricted the availability of external support. As a result, in Egypt, Jordan, and Tunisia, economic indicators are presently flashing yellow, and macroeconomic crises with sharp currency depreciation and banking crises are possible in the future. IMF programs are being developed in these countries, but the "street" may not allow the passage of minimal reform programs that can contain deficits to levels that are financeable (let alone sustainable). By the beginning of 2013, it had become clear that economic recovery could not proceed until the political crises were resolved. Indeed, a downward spiral may ensue as polarized politics exacerbate economic difficulties, in turn leading to more fractious politics.

While in opposition, the Islamist movements that came to power in Egypt and Tunisia had frequently criticized the economic policies of the previous regimes and had promised to combat corruption, poverty, and inequality. In the face of the political turmoil generated by the rush to fill the power vacuum, write constitutions, and compete for elections, however, Islamists have been unable to move on any of their big promises. Their commitments to promoting social justice, reducing subsidies in order to provide more fiscal space in budgets, attacking cronyism, and eliminating waste in bloated bureaucracies have not been realized thus far.

Going Forward: Economic Reforms for the Future

The political and economic challenges facing the Arab transitioning countries are compounded by high popular expectations and problematic legacies of the past. How political challenges are addressed will largely determine the course of economic policies. Unless new surprises arise, the contours of the emerging political settlement will include fewer favors for elite capital. Yet new rulers should attempt to make peace with large capital-holders and convince them to invest in the future, as is already happening in Egypt, rather than withdraw, as happened with the socialist revolutions of the 1960s. At the same time, the interests of the poor should be balanced with those of the middle classes, which benefited disproportionately under authoritarian bargains.

Certain technical challenges will remain difficult to resolve, even if politics become less polarized. The first and most immediate challenge is economic stabilization in order to avoid an economic and financial meltdown, which would further complicate the political process. Building a package of measures that reduce expenditures, raise revenues, and command some minimum level of popular support is a tricky endeavor in the best of circumstances, and it will be very challenging in the current hyperpoliticized environment. A more stable political environment, however, also offers the possibility of initiating other important reforms over the next three to five years.

The second area of focus should be the modernization of the state and the rehabilitation of public services, especially health, education, and social protection. New governments with broad popular support should be able to redirect expenditures toward social services and away from subsidies that benefit the better-off and to make tax systems more progressive while enlarging the tax base. Improving service delivery and fighting petty corruption will require increases in public-sector wages, which will be complicated by the large size of the civil service, particularly in Egypt.

The third agenda concerns the business environment and job creation. Past experiences, and especially the failures of both socialism and state capitalism, limit policy choices for the Arab region. For example, developing an effective industrial policy that supports rising sectors of the economy with targeted subsidies, as was done in East Asia, would be an unreasonable goal in the next three to five years, given institutional weaknesses and the risks of capture by powerful interest groups. Priority issues such as improving competition, democratizing credit, and reducing the constraints faced by the informal sector do not have easy solutions.

These are complicated challenges, technically, politically, and administratively. In the end, what will make a difference is the process by which solutions adapted to the particular environments of each country are found and implemented. The greatest contribution of the "revolutions" to these challenges should be in fostering greater popular participation in the policymaking process. It is the sense of empowerment of new actors such as labor unions, employers' associations, student groups, and other civil society groups—who can cross ideological lines to represent social interests and hold their representatives accountable—that constitutes the real revolution.

NOTES

1. See Pepinsky (2009) and Slater (2010) on the importance of coalitions for authoritarian durability.

2. In 2005, the percentage of the population living on $2 per day was about 17% in the Middle East and Latin America, 39% in East Asia, 73% in sub-Saharan Africa, and 74% in South Asia. When measured by the percentage of the population living on $1.25 per day, the Middle East has by far the lowest poverty rate of all regions (World Bank, *World Development Indicators*, 2005).

3. For example, the share of the informal sector in the economy was 44% in Morocco, 33% in Egypt, 34% in Syria, 30% in Tunisia and Lebanon, and 26% in Jordan. This is higher than the share in many developing countries, such as Indonesia and Vietnam, where the informal sector accounts for about 21% and 16% of the economy, respectively. In the United States, the informal sector accounts for about 9% of the economy (World Bank, *World Development Indicators*, 2010).

4. For example, public spending on education as a percentage of GDP has hovered around 5% since the late 1970s (World Bank, *World Development Indicators*, various years).

5. For reviews of this literature, see Posusney and Angrist (2005) and Schlumberger (2007).

6. For example, spending on energy subsidies exceeds social expenditures by two to three times in Egypt and Tunisia.

7. In Egypt, real wages in the public sector declined over time. The minimum wage, which anchors all wages, declined from 60% of per capita GDP in the early 1980s to a mere 13% in 2007 (Abdelhamid and El Baradei 2009).

8. Data from the World Values Survey also suggest that the average financial satisfaction of the poor has deteriorated, that of the middle classes remains stable, and that of the rich has risen, further bolstering a sense of rising inequality during the period (Diwan 2013).

9. In 2000, however, young people were much more likely to support democracy than their elders (Diwan 2013).

10. Between 1998 and 2006, according to household surveys, GDP rose by 60% in nominal terms, while consumption stayed essentially at the same level all along the distribution, suggesting that large parts of the increase may have accrued to the undercounted rich and that very little has trickled down to the rest of society.

11. In Egypt, average years of education had risen from two years in the 1980s to eight years by 2009 (Barro and Lee 2010; Campante and Chor 2011).

12. The plight of the main character of the novel *The Yacoubian Building*, written by the Egyptian author and dentist Alaa al-Aswany (2006), shows poignantly the frustration of

well-educated youth whose families lack the social standing and relationships to enable them to realize their professional aspirations.

13. During the sustained protests in Tahrir Square that led to Mubarak's resignation, the Muslim Brotherhood and other Islamist groups (along with other non-Islamist citizen groups) helped to solve the coordination problems that constrain social mobilization by opening up mosques as meeting points and medical treatment centers.

14. Similar processes of moderation took place in Turkey and Tunisia. In Turkey, a combination of the lessons from repression, opportunism, and the growth of a friendly middle class compelled the AKP to moderate (Demiralp 2009; Mecham 2004). In Tunisia, the Al-Nahda leadership claimed in 1981, "We have no right to interpose between the people and those whom the people choose and elect" (Tamimi 2001).

15. In Egypt, state repression increased after the electoral gains of the Muslim Brotherhood in the 2005 elections. When the party emerged as a credible alternative, the ruling regime cracked down on it more forcefully (Osman 2010).

16. For example, the Deauville Partnership, an international effort launched by the G8 countries in May 2011, aimed to provide assistance for economic stabilization, job creation, good governance, and regional integration in the Arab transitioning countries.

REFERENCES

Abdelhamid, Doha, and El Baradei, Laila (2009), "Reforming the Pay System for Government Employees in Egypt," Working paper, Cairo, Government of Egypt, Information and Decision Support Center.

Abouleinem, Soheir, Al-Tathy, Heba, and Kheir-el-Din, Hanaa (2009), *The Impact of Phasing Out the Petroleum Subsidies in Egypt,* Working Paper no. 145, Cairo, Egypt, Egyptian Center for Economic Studies.

Ahram Online (2011), "Cairo Gated Community Palm Hills Found Illegal," Ahram Online, March 1.

Alley, April Longley (2010), "The Rules of the Game: Unpacking Patronage Politics in Yemen," *Middle East Journal,* 64, 3, 385–409.

ASDA'A/Burson-Marsteller (2010), *Arab Youth Survey 2009/2010,* Dubai, UAE, ASDA'A/ Burson-Marsteller.

Assaad, Ragui (2009), "Labor Supply, Employment, and Unemployment in the Egyptian Economy, 1988–2006," in *The Egyptian Labor Market Revisited,* ed. Ragui Assaad, Cairo, Egypt, American University in Cairo.

_____ (2011), *The Structure and Evolution of Employment in Jordan,* Minneapolis and St. Paul, University of Minnesota.

Al Aswany, Alaa (2006), *The Yacoubian Building: A Novel,* New York, Harper Perennial.

El Badawi, Ibrahim, and Makdisi, Samir (2007), "Explaining the Democracy Deficit in the Arab World," *Quarterly Review of Economics and Finance,* 46, 813–831.

Barro, Robert J., and Lee, Jong-Wha Lee (2010), "A New Data Set of Educational Attainment in the World, 1950–2010," Working Paper no. 15902, Cambridge, National Bureau of Economic Research.

Beaugé, Florence (2011), "Orange Tunisie Passe sous la Tutelle de l'État Tunisien," *Le Monde,* March 30, 18.

Belhaj, Nadia, and Wissa, Christiane (2011), "Inequality Trends and Determinants in the Arab Region," paper presented at the conference "Inequality in the Arab Region," Economic Research Forum (ERF), Cairo, Egypt.

Bellin, Eva (2004), "The Robustness of Authoritarianism in the Middle East: Exceptionalism in Comparative Perspective," *Comparative Politics*, 36, 2, 139–157.

Benchemsi, Ahmed (2012), "Morocco: Outfoxing the Opposition," *Journal of Democracy*, 23, 1, 57–69.

Bibi, Sami, and Nabli, Mustapha K. (2011), "Equity and Inequality in the Arab Region," Policy Research Report, Cairo, Egypt, Economic Research Forum (ERF).

Browers, Michaelle L. (2009), *Political Ideology in the Arab World: Accommodation and Transformation*, Cambridge, Cambridge University Press.

Brubaker, Rogers (2006), *Ethnicity Without Groups*, Cambridge, Harvard University Press.

Burgat, François (2003), *Face to Face with Political Islam*, London, I. B. Tauris.

Cammett, Melani (2007), *Globalization and Business Politics in Arab North Africa: A Comparative Perspective*, Cambridge, Cambridge University Press.

Campante, Filipe R., and Chor, Davin (2011), "'The People Want the Fall of the Regime': Schooling, Political Protest, and the Economy," Faculty Research Working Paper Series, Cambridge, Harvard University, John F. Kennedy School of Government.

Catusse, Myriam (2008), *Le Temps des Entrepreneurs? Politique et Transformations du Capitalisme au Maroc*, Paris, Maisonneuve & Larose.

Chandra, Kanchan, ed. (2012), *Constructivist Theories of Ethnic Politics*, Oxford, Oxford University Press.

Chekir, Hamouda, and Diwan, Ishac (2012), "Distressed Whales on the Nile—Egypt Capitalists in the Wake of the 2010 Revolution," Working Paper no. 250, Cambridge, Harvard University, Center for International Development.

Cingranelli-Richards (CIRI) (various years), *Human Rights Dataset.*

Confédération Démocratique du Travail (CDT)/Cofitex (1997), Fes, Morocco, Barnamig Ittifaq.

Demiralp, Seda (2009), "The Rise of Islamic Capital and the Decline of Islamic Radicalism in Turkey," *Comparative Politics*, 41, 3, 315–335.

Dillman, Bradford (2000), *State and Private Sector in Algeria: The Politics of Rent-Seeking and Failed Development*, Boulder, Westview Press.

Diwan, Ishac (2013), "Who Are the Democrats? Leading Opinions in the Wake of Egypt's 2011 Popular Uprisings," Cambridge, Harvard University, John F. Kennedy School of Government.

Esping-Andersen, Gøsta (1990), *Three Worlds of Welfare Capitalism*, Princeton, Princeton University Press.

Esposito, John L. (1997), *Political Islam: Revolution, Radicalism, or Reform?* Boulder, Colo., Lynne Rienner Publishers.

Fearon, James D., and Laitin, David D. (1996), "Explaining Interethnic Cooperation," *American Political Science Review*, 90, 4, 715–735.

Fuller, Graham (2004), *The Future of Political Islam*, New York, Palgrave Macmillan.

Gumuscu, Sebnem, and Sert, Deniz (2009), "The Power of the Devout Bourgeoisie: The Case of the Justice and Development Party in Turkey," *Middle Eastern Studies*, 45, 6, 953–968.

Haddad, Bassam (2012), *Business Networks in Syria: The Political Economy of Authoritarian Resilience,* Stanford, Stanford University Press.

Henry, Clement M. (1996), *The Mediterranean Debt Crescent: Money and Power in Algeria, Egypt, Morocco, Tunisia, and Turkey,* Gainesville, University Press of Florida.

Hertog, Steffen (2010), *Princes, Brokers, and Bureaucrats: Oil and the State in Saudi Arabic,* Ithaca, Cornell University Press.

Heydemann, Steven, ed. (2004), *Networks of Privilege in the Middle East: The Politics of Economic Reform Revisited,* New York, Palgrave Macmillan.

Hibou, Beatrice (2006), *La Force de L'Obeissance: Economic Politique de la Repression en Tunisie,* Paris, Editions de la Decouverte.

Imam, Patrick A., and Jacobs, Davina F. (2007), *Effect of Corruption on Tax Revenues in the Middle East,* Working Paper, Washington, D.C., International Monetary Fund.

IMF (International Monetary Fund) (2013), *Energy Subsidy Reforms: Lessons and Implications,* Washington, D.C., IMF.

Jabar, Faleh (2003), *The Shiite Movement in Iraq,* London, Saqi Books.

Kaboub, Fadhel (2012), "From Neoliberalism to Social Justice: The Feasibility of Full Employment in Tunisia," *Review of Radical Political Economics,* 44, 3, 305–312.

Kang, David (2002), *Crony Capitalism: Corruption and Development in South Korea and the Philippines,* Cambridge, Cambridge University Press.

Kar, Dev, and Curcio, Karly (2011), *Illicit Financial Flows from Developing Countries: 2000–2009: Update with a Focus on Asia,* Washington, D.C., Global Financial Integrity.

Karshenas, Massoud, and Moghadam, Valentine M., eds. (2006), *Social Policy in the Middle East: Economic, Political, and Gender Dynamics,* New York, United Nations Research Institute for Social Development and Palgrave Macmillan.

Khan, Mushtaq H. (2010), *Political Settlements and the Governance of Growth-Enhancing Institutions,* London, School of Oriental and African Studies (SOAS).

Kienle, Eberhard (2001), *A Grand Delusion: Democracy and Economic Reform in Egypt,* London, I. B. Tauris.

_____ (2002), *Contemporary Syria: Liberalization Between Cold War and Cold Peace,* London, University of London, Centre of Near and Middle Eastern Studies.

Levitsky, Steven, and Way, Lucan A. (2010), *Competitive Authoritarianism: Hybrid Regimes After the Cold War,* Cambridge, Cambridge University Press.

Lieberman, Evan S., and Singh, Prerna (2012), "Conceptualizing and Measuring Ethnic Politics: An Institutional Complement to Demographic, Behavioral, and Cognitive Approaches," *Studies in Comparative International Development,* 47, 3, 255–286.

Lust, Ellen (2011), "Missing the Third Wave: Islam, Institutions, and Democracy in the Middle East," *Studies in Comparative International Development,* 46, 2, 163–190.

Mares, Isabela (2003), *The Politics of Social Risk: Business and Welfare State Development,* Cambridge, Cambridge University Press.

Marshall, Shana, and Stacher, Joshua (2012), "Egypt's Generals and Transnational Capital," *Middle East Report,* Winter.

Massad, Joseph (2001), *Colonial Effects: The Making of National Identity in Jordan,* New York, Columbia University Press.

McAdam, Doug (1982), *Political Process and the Development of Black Insurgency, 1930–1970,* Chicago, University of Chicago Press.

Mecham, R. Quinn (2004), "From the Ashes of Virtue, a Promise of Light: The Transformation of Political Islam in Turkey," *Third World Quarterly,* 25, 2, 339–358.

Moore, Pete (2004), *Doing Business in the Middle East: Politics and Economic Crisis in Jordan and Kuwait,* Cambridge, Cambridge University Press.

Nasr, Seyyed Vali Reza (2009), *Forces of Fortune: The Rise of the New Muslim Middle Class and What It Will Mean for Our World,* New York, Simon & Schuster.

Noland, Marcus, and Pack, Howard (2007), *The Arab Economies in a Changing World,* Washington, D.C., Peterson Institute for International Economics.

Osman, Tarek (2010), *Egypt on the Brink: From Nasser to Mubarak,* New Haven, Yale University Press.

Pepinsky, Thomas B. (2009), *Economic Crises and the Breakdown of Authoritarian Regimes: Indonesia and Malaysia in Comparative Perspective,* Cambridge, Cambridge University Press.

Pew Research Center Report (2011), "Arab Spring Fails to Improve US Image," Washington, DC, Pew Research, Global Attitudes Project.

Posusney, Marsha Pripstein, and Angrist, Michele Penner (2005), *Authoritarianism in the Middle East: Regimes and Resistance,* Boulder, Lynne Rienner Publishers.

Roll, Steven (2010), "'Finance Matters!' The Influence of Financial Sector Reforms on the Development of the Entrepreneurial Elite in Egypt," *Mediterranean Politics,* 15, 349–370.

Saadowski, Yahya M. (1991), *Political Vegetables? Businessman and Bureaucrat in the Development of Egyptian Agriculture,* Washington, D.C., Brookings.

Salehi-Isfahani, Djavad, Belhaj, Nadia, and Assaad, Ragui (2011), "Equality of Opportunity in Education in the Middle East and North Africa," Cairo, Egypt, Economic Research Forum (ERF).

Schlumberger, Oliver, ed. (2007), *Debating Arab Authoritarianism: Dynamics and Durability in Nondemocratic Regimes,* Stanford, Stanford University Press.

Sfakianakis, John (2004), "The Whales of the Nile: Networks, Businessmen, and Bureaucrats During the Era of Privatization in Egypt," in *Networks of Privilege: Rethinking the Politics of Economic Reform in the Middle East,* ed. S. Heydemann, New York, Palgrave Macmillan.

Shahin, Emad El-Din (2005), "Political Islam: Ready for Engagement?" Working Paper, Madrid, Spain, Fundación para las Relaciones Internacionales y el Diálogo Exterior (FRIDE).

Slater, Dan (2010), *Ordering Power: Contentious Politics and Authoritarian Leviathans in Southeast Asia,* Cambridge, Cambridge University Press.

Tamimi, Azzam S. (2001), *Rachid Ghannouchi: A Democrat Within Islamism,* Oxford, Oxford University Press.

Tessler, Mark (2011), *Public Opinion in the Middle East: Survey Research and the Political Orientations of Ordinary Citizens,* Bloomington, Indiana University Press.

Tlemcani, Rachid (1999), *État, Bazar, et Globalisation: L'Aventure de l'Infitah en Algérie,* Algiers, Les Editions El-Hikma.

Vandewalle, Dirk (1998), *Libya Since Independence: Oil and State-Building,* Ithaca, Cornell University Press.

Vitalis, Robert (2007), *America's Kingdom: Mythmaking on the Saudi Oil Frontier,* Stanford, Calif., Stanford University Press.

World Bank (2005), *World Development Indicators,* at http://data.worldbank.org/data-catalog /world-development-indicators.

_____ (2009), *From Privilege to Competition: Unlocking Private-Led Growth in the Middle East and North Africa,* Washington, D.C., World Bank.

_____ (2010), *World Development Indicators,* at http://data.worldbank.org/data-catalog /world-development-indicators.

Yom, Sean L., and Gause, F. Gregory, III (2012), "Resilient Royals: How Arab Monarchies Hang On," *Journal of Democracy,* 23, 4, 74–88.

Yousef, Tarik M. (2004), "Development, Growth, and Policy Reform in the Middle East and North Africa Since 1950," *Journal of Economic Perspectives,* 18, 3, 91–116.

Zogby International (2005), *Attitudes of Arabs: An In-Depth Look at Social and Political Concerns of Arabs,* Washington, D.C., Arab American Institute.

INDEX

CPSIA information can be obtained
at www.ICGtesting.com
Printed in the USA
LVHW090205141019
634106LV00001B/45/P